GIANT'S CAUSEWAY

AND OTHER INCREDIBLE NATURAL WONDERS

TIM COOKE

Lerner Publications ◆ Minneapolis

Lerner Publications Company
An imprint of Lerner Publishing Group, Inc.
241 First Avenue North
Minneapolis, MN 55401 USA

For reading levels and more information, look up this title at www.lernerbooks.com.

Main body text set in Aptifer Sans LT Pro 14/18.
Typeface provided by Linotype.

Library of Congress Cataloging-in-Publication Data

Names: Cooke, Tim, 1961–author.
Title: Giant's causeway and other incredible natural wonders / Tim Cooke.
Description: Minneapolis : Lerner Publications, [2024] | Series: Ultimate adventure guides |
    Includes bibliographical references and index. | Audience: Ages 8–11 | Audience: Grades 4–6 |
    Summary: "From the hottest deserts to the depths of the ocean, Earth boasts some amazing
    natural wonders. Engaging text and colorful photographs bring excitement to these incredible
    geological phenomena"—Provided by publisher.
Identifiers: LCCN 2023015989 (print) | LCCN 2023015990 (ebook) | ISBN 9798765609200
    (library binding) | ISBN 9798765625071 (paperback) | ISBN 9798765618547 (epub)
Subjects: LCSH: Natural history—Juvenile literature.
Classification: LCC QH48 .C64 2024 (print) | LCC QH48 (ebook) | DDC
508—dc23/eng/20230605

LC record available at https://lccn.loc.gov/2023015989
LC ebook record available at https://lccn.loc.gov/2023015990

Manufactured in the United States of America
1 – CG – 12/15/23

Table of Contents

Chapter 1

REMARKABLE ROCKS

All around the world are signs of how Earth has been formed over millions of years. Some clues lie in spectacular rock formations.

Giant's Causeway, Northern Ireland

People used to think the Giant's Causeway was not formed by nature. The causeway has more than forty thousand pillars of rock, each with six sides. The stones lead out into the sea like stepping stones. The pillars fit together so closely it looks as if someone tried to build a path from Northern Ireland to Scotland. For people in the past, there was only one explanation: giants!

A causeway is a raised route above wet or flooded ground—just as the rocks appear!

The rock pillars fit together perfectly.

In fact, the rock pillars were created when a volcano erupted about fifty to sixty million years ago. Hot, molten rock, or lava, flowed into the sea and cooled. It created a rock called basalt. The basalt formed very irregular shapes.

Traveler's Checklist ✓

✓ **Wear hiking boots.** The coast is rocky and uneven, so you need a good grip to walk over the rocks.

✓ **Take a coat and some sunblock.** This part of Northern Ireland is famous for having weather that changes often!

Zangye National Geopark, China

If you think rocks are always gray or brown, think again. The rocks in Zangye National Geopark are purples, blues, and golds. The bands of rocks form striped patterns. The rocks were formed underwater. Grains of sand and mud settled at the bottom of the water and hardened into a rock called sandstone.

Millions of years later, movement of rocks in the ground pushed the sandstone up into the air. Wind and rain began to wear away the rock. Today, Zangye has rock towers, tall ridges, and deep ravines.

The colored rocks at Zangye stretch over 100 square miles (260 sq km).

NATURAL FORCES AT WORK

Zangye was created by two natural forces. The first is called stratification. When grains of sand sink to the seafloor, they are squeezed into a soft type of rock. Over time, they form layers called strata. The second force is called erosion. Wind and rain wear away the soft sandstone. That creates shapes including towers, cones, and even arches.

Bryce Canyon, Utah

One of the first people who visited Bryce Canyon was a farmer. He called it "a heck of a place to lose a cow." Hundreds of rock towers called hoodoos reach up to the skies. They crowd together, like trees in a forest. It's easy to get lost there.

The pink rocks of Bryce Canyon were formed millions of years ago. Earthquakes pushed them up to the surface. There, the rain, snow, and wind shaped the soft rock into pillars. Harder rocks were left behind, balancing on top of the hoodoos like hats.

The tallest hoodoo at Bryce Canyon is about 200 feet (60 m) tall.

Chapter 2

WONDERFUL WATER

More than seventy percent of Earth's surface is covered in water. It's no wonder that some of the most incredible places on the planet were created by water or beneath the ocean.

Great Barrier Reef, Australia

This coral reef is so big it can be seen from space. It is made up of nine hundred small islands and two thousand five hundred reefs. A reef may look like it is made of rock, but it is really made from tiny animals called corals. When the corals die, their hard shells form rocky reefs.

Reefs provide many other animals with food and shelter. The reef is home to four hundred types of coral. There are also one thousand five hundred types of fish and four thousand types of shellfish. The water is warm and full of sunlight. Reefs are beautiful but deadly. Many of the animals eat each other to survive.

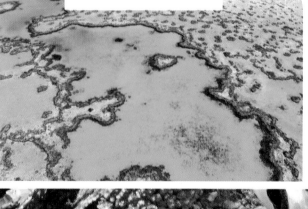

The reefs form shallow lagoons of warm, clear water ideal for many creatures to live.

CORAL REEFS UNDER THREAT

Many coral reefs are dying. Corals grow best in water that is warm and clean. They need sunlight to live. Climate change means that sea levels are rising. That makes the water deeper, so it is cooler. In addition, pollution from the land makes the water dirty. When coral dies, there is less food for animals living on the reef.

The white rocks form a series of step-like terraces.

Pamukkale, Turkey

In Turkish, Pamukkale means the "Cotton Palace." The rocks that surround the turquoise pools of water look like they are made of cotton wool. The white rocks are so bright they hurt your eyes in the sunshine.

The pools at Pamukkale are formed by underground springs. Warm water bubbles flow out of the hillside. The water carries minerals that settle and slowly form solid rock. Some of the rocks look like frozen waterfalls. Others look like stone trees.

For more than two thousand five hundred years, people have been taking a dip in the warm water. They believe the minerals are good for their health.

Great Blue Hole, Belize

As you sail near the Great Blue Hole, the clear water turns dark blue. You're passing over an underwater hole nearly 1,000 feet (305 m) across. The bottom of the hole is 400 feet (120 m) deep, so it is always dark. The hole was created when the seafloor was still dry land. Over time, water dripped into the rock. It hollowed out many caves. Those caves collapsed into a single hole. When the sea level rose, water flowed into the hole.

Traveler's Checklist ☑

☑ **Travel by boat.** It's the only way to get to the lonely island location.

☑ **Bring your diving gear.** The Great Blue Hole attracts divers from all over the world.

BC20983

Ger
* 25.
DEPAR

MALAYSIA
KLIA 2
25.03.15
DEC 16

Spain ✈
04/10/16
ARRIVAL

ARRIVAL MAY

MAR
14

16 Paris
OCT France
INTERNATIONAL AIRPORT
JKE6
1355
3568

SA ✈
C 16

Chapter 3

DRAMATIC DESERTS

Deserts are the hottest, driest places on Earth. They look as if nothing can live there, but you might be surprised. Many animals have adapted to the harsh conditions.

Death Valley, California

Death Valley was named by settlers heading for California. A few springs bring water up from the ground. Minerals in the water create crusty, white salt flats. Another part of the valley is full of tall sand dunes. Tall peaks of colored rocks look out over the valley.

Death Valley is actually full of life. Humans have lived here for centuries. Now, they visit as tourists. The valley is home to coyotes, ground squirrels, lizards, and rattlesnakes. When it rains, flowers bloom in the desert.

The floor of Death Valley is covered by white salt flats and sand.

Skeleton Coast, Namibia

The Skeleton Coast is an unusual desert. It stretches along the coast of the Atlantic Ocean, but very little water from the ocean moves inland. Heavy waves crash onto the beach and thick fog hangs in the air.

Wrecked ships lie all along the coast.

Many ships have been stranded here when sailors lost their way in the fog. The desert gets its name from the many animal bones lying in the sand. Most of the bones came from whales that were hunted and harvested on the beach.

The wind blows from the land toward the sea. It prevents any moisture from the sea moving inland.

Singing Dunes, Gobi Desert

Over a thousand years ago, an Italian explorer named Marco Polo became the first European to travel to China. To get there, he crossed through the Gobi Desert. At night, the air was full of low rumbling noises. It sounded as though the sand was singing! Polo was frightened. He thought the noise was coming from the spirits of dead people.

Today, we know that the desert really does make a noise, but not because of spirits. The desert is made up of grains of sand. When the wind blows, it makes the grains of sand near the surface vibrate. When the grains all vibrate at the same time, they make a booming sound. The sound is higher or lower depending on how fast the grains are moving.

Traveler's Checklist ✓

✓ **Bring water.** It's very hot in the daytime, so you should carry about 1 gallon (4.5 l) per person for one day.

✓ **Pack a coat and gloves.** At night, the desert gets very cold.

In order to sing, dunes
have to be large and
dry, with just the right
shaped grains of sand.

Chapter 4

GREEN TREASURES

In some places, the landscape and the climate combine to make the perfect conditions for life. In rainforests, trees grow hundreds of feet tall. On the open plains, grass stretches as far as the eye can see.

Everglades, Florida

The southern tip of Florida is covered in grass and forests, but if you try to walk there, you'll get wet feet. The whole area is covered in swamps and slow-moving rivers. These are the Everglades. They are very flat, so the water does not flow off to the ocean.

The swampy land is home to mangrove trees with large roots that stretch out into the swamps. Vast prairies of sawgrass grow in the shallow water. Many animals live in the Everglades, including alligators and crocodiles. Protecting the Everglades is essential to saving species such as the Florida panther and the manatee.

About two hundred thousand alligators live in the Everglades.

Amazon Rainforest, Brazil

The rainforest that spreads over the basin of the Amazon River in Brazil is home to the greatest diversity of animal and plant life on the planet. The warm, wet climate helps huge trees grow high into the air. Their top leaves form a canopy above the forest below, where many other smaller plants grow. There are plants, birds, mammals, reptiles, and insects here that do not exist anywhere else. Indigenous peoples still live in the forest.

After rain, warm steam rises from the rainforest.

Experts think that the forest may be home to plants and animals that have not yet been discovered. If this is true, some of them could save people's lives. Scientists may be able to use them to make medicines that could protect people from certain diseases.

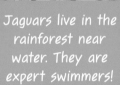

Jaguars live in the rainforest near water. They are expert swimmers!

Thick vegetation lines a creek in the Daintree Forest.

Daintree Forest, Australia

There has been a tropical rainforest on the coast of Australia for millions of years. The Daintree Forest is home to some of the earliest plants that appeared on Earth as life evolved. These ancient plants include giant ferns, tall conifers or fir trees, and flowering plants. This forest is a reminder of how forests used to look when dinosaurs roamed the Earth.

Mangrove trees have roots that lift them off the ground, like stilts.

Traveler's Checklist ☑

☑ **Carry bug spray.** There are all sorts of biting insects in the Daintree Forest, so it's best to protect yourself.

☑ **Wear long sleeved shirts and long pants.** They will protect you against bugs and poisonous plants.

☑ **Pack a raincoat.** It is almost always raining in the forest!

BC20983

Ger
✱ 25.
DEPAR

MALAYSIA
KLIA 2
25.03.15

Spain ✈
04/10/16
ARRIVAL

BRAZIL IMMIGRATION
MAR
14

USA ✈
IGRATION
16

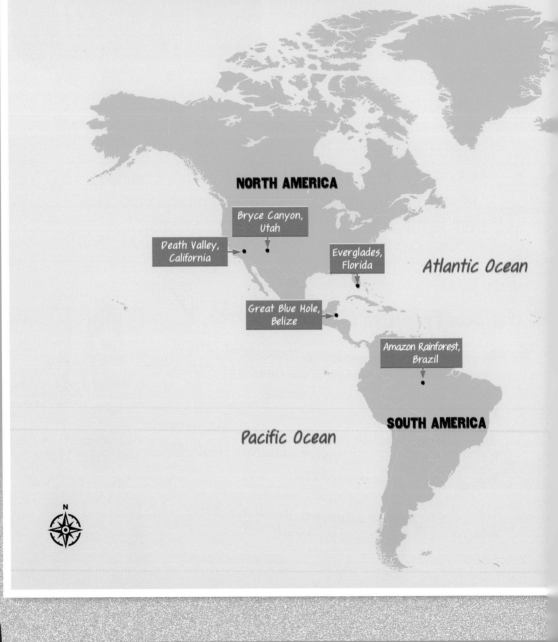

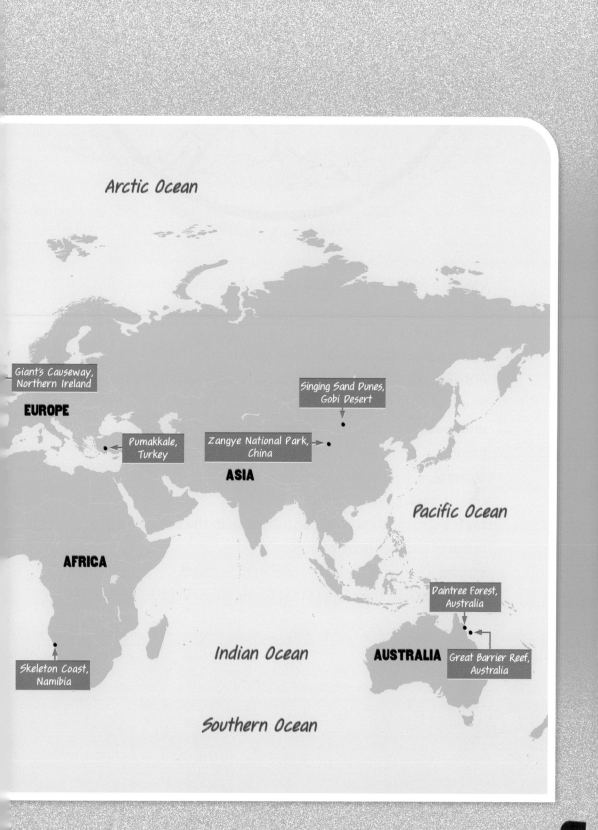

Arctic Ocean

Giant's Causeway,
Northern Ireland

EUROPE

Pumakkale,
Turkey

Zangye National Park,
China

Singing Sand Dunes,
Gobi Desert

ASIA

Pacific Ocean

AFRICA

Daintree Forest,
Australia

Indian Ocean

AUSTRALIA

Great Barrier Reef,
Australia

Skeleton Coast,
Namibia

Southern Ocean

basin: a hollow area of land drained by a river system

climate change: changes in the climate and weather patterns that are happening because of human activity

dune: a sand hill formed by wind or tides

erosion: the wearing away of something by wind or water

hoodoo: a column of rock that has been shaped by erosion

indigenous: coming from or naturally occurring in a particular place

mineral: a solid substance found in the earth that does not come from a plant or animal

reef: a strip of coral, sand, or rock close to the surface of the ocean or another body of water

strata: a series of layers of rocks in the ground

stratification: the process that forms strata in rocks

Learn More

Boynton, Alice, and Wiley Blevins, *Let It Rain: Exploring the Amazon Rain Forest*. South Egremont, MA: Red Chair Press, 2018.

Department of the Interior, Death Valley
https://www.doi.gov/blog/12-things-you-didnt-know-about-death-valley

London, Martha. *Giant's Causeway*. Minneapolis: Abdo Publishing, 2021.

Martin, Claudia. *Coral Reefs*. Minneapolis: QEB Publishing. 2020.

National Geographic Kids, Deserts
https://kids.nationalgeographic.com/nature/habitats/article/desert

National Park Service, Bryce Canyon
https://www.nps.gov/brca/learn/nature/hoodoos.htm

Index

Photo Acknowledgments

Image credits: RomanSlavik.com/Shutterstock.com, p. 1; Sergii Figurnyi/Shutterstock.com, p. 5; LMspencer/
Shutterstock.com, p. 6a; Lars Poyansky/Shutterstock.com, pp. 6b, 15b, 20b, 27b; MarijaPiliponyte/
Shutterstock.com, p. 6c; Creative Stall/Shutterstock.com, p. 6d; Jeroen Mikkers/Shutterstock.com, p. 7;
Tetyana Dotsenko/Shutterstock.com, p. 9a; Sean Pavone/Shutterstock.com, p. 9b; V_E/Shutterstock.
com, p. 11a; marcobrivio.photography/Shutterstock.com, p. 11b; Rich Carey/Shutterstock.com, p. 12;
muratart/Shutterstock.com, p. 13; Kota Irie/Shutterstock.com, p. 14; curiosity/Shutterstock.com, p. 15a;
Gennady Stetsenko/Shutterstock.com, p. 17; Smelov/Shutterstock.com, pp. 18–19; Lukas Bischoff
Photograph/Shutterstock.com, pp. 18b; BNP Design Studio/Shutterstock.com, p. 20a; Kondrachov Vladimir/
Shutterstock.com, p. 21; Melissa King/Shutterstock.com, p. 23; Al'fred/Shutterstock.com, pp. 24–25;
Mark Green/Shutterstock.com, p. 25; AustralianCamera/Shutterstock.com, p. 26; Stephen Bridger/
Shutterstock.com, p. 27a; inspiring.team/Shutterstock.com, p. 27c; Sabelskaya/Shutterstock.com, p. 27d;
Andrei Minsk/Shutterstock.com, pp. 28–29; Cover: Sergii Figurnyi/Shutterstock.com.